Kick The Wor

Take Back Control of your Life

By Lynne Daly

Introduction

we humans, seem to worry all the time, about everything under the sun; we worry about our jobs, families, relationships and even our future, and by allowing all this space in the mind to be took up with negative thoughts can really take a toll on your happiness and even on your ability to live your life the way you want it to be, because you are being constantly blocked by your anxiety and the habit of worrying over every little thing that comes your way. It's something we find ourselves all doing and it is not something to be ashamed of, but it is something that you should try to keep in check, for your own sake and the people in your close circle. At the end of the day, worrying over something, that you can't control its outcome and you are almost certainly torturing yourself over absolutely nothing.

The bottom line in this problem is precisely the inherent futility of your mental gymnastics, because while you imagine hundreds of different things you could have done differently or ways in which a situation could descend into chaos, in the real world, life goes on, as usual, with absolutely no interference caused by your thoughts.

Worrying is not something that you will ever win from and it is, in fact, a source of constant stress, irritation, anxiety and even illness, in its most severe forms. Negative thinking and pessimism have been proven to be detrimental to our mental and physical health and to our overall happiness, so the best thing you can do for yourself is to eliminate your negative thoughts. It is completely doable, and all you need is a little guidance. Luckily, this e-book was written with the purpose of helping people who are struggling with negative thinking and worrying too much. You need to stop it from taking over your life and this e-book is your definite guide to achieving a happier life with significantly less negative thinking. By following the steps outlined here, you will be able to change the way you approach your problems and learn to "train" yourself to stop thinking negatively.

Table of Contents

Chapter 1- Most of The Thing's You Worry About Don't Happen

Over five hundred years ago, Michel de Montaigne said: "My life has been filled with terrible misfortune; most of which never happened."

Now there is a study that has proved it. This study looked into how many of our imagined calamities never did materialize. In this study, subjects were asked to write down their worries over an extended period of time and then identify which of their imagined misfortunes didn't actually happen. Low and behold, it turns out that 86 percent of what subjects worried about never happened, and with the 14 percent that did happen, 79 percent of subjects discovered either they could handle the difficulty better than expected, or the difficulty taught them a lesson worth learning. This means that 97 percent of what you worry over is nothing more than a fearful mind punishing you with exaggerations and misperceptions.

Montaigne's quote may have made people laugh for five centuries, but worry is, however, no joke. The stress it generates can cause serious mental and physical problems. The stress hormones that worry dumps into your brain have been linked to shrinking brain mass, lowering your IQ, being prone to heart disease, cancer, and premature aging, predicting marital problems, family dysfunction, and clinical depression, and making seniors more likely to develop dementia and Alzheimer's.

If we could get a grip on the worry that habitually, incessantly, and often unconsciously seizes hold of our mind, we would, of course, increase the odds of living a longer, happier, and more successful life. But don't worry; new research has found that you can rewire your brain to stop worrying. It starts with the decision not to believe the misfortune that your worried thoughts see in your future. An example of someone who made that decision is an elderly man my father   was asked to drive to the clinic for an annual check-up.

My father didn't know this man. All he was told was that this person was more than 90 years old and probably quite frail. But the person who opened the door when he knocked could hardly be described as old and frail. The person who stood before him was a sprightly man who appeared to be in his seventies at the very most.

"Do you mind me asking how old you are?" my father asked on the drive to the doctor.

"93," the man answered.

My father was astonished. "You look so much younger," he said. "What's your secret?"

"Well, my friend," he answered, "30 years ago I made the decision to stop worrying and I haven't wasted a moment on worry since."

It was this decision that made him younger and healthier than his chronological age. Think of all the energy he gained through his decision not to worry. Think of all the anxiety he spared himself, all the needless stress he avoided. My Father said that it showed on his face, in his attitude, and in how well his brain functioned.

It's possible to make this same choice to let go of worry and gradually move past worry altogether. You can rewire your brain to quiet the worry habit. It takes a decision and it takes a special kind of practice, but it's simpler than you could imagine.

Nature has given us a small but helpful 90-second window to stop stressful thinking before it takes a long walk off a short pier,in that 90 seconds, you have the choice to kill the worry,press the Clear button in your mind and focus on solutions or let worry take control of you. The more you put a stop to stressful thinking during the day, the more your brain will strengthen synapses that end worry.

Here is the neurological reason why the Clear Button works. The part of the brain that causes stress reactions literally has the intelligence of a toddler. And every parent knows you don't stop a tantrum by appealing to a child's logic. You need to distract the child. This tool distracts the terrible two-year-old in your brain from casting you off the deep end.

Another simple approach to dissolving worry is called "Finish Each Day and Be Done With It." It allows you the choice to let go of the day's problems, so you don't take them home. This piece of wisdom comes from a letter written by the great American philosopher, Ralph Waldo Emerson, to his daughter who was worried over a mistake she'd made. This is what it says:

"Finish each day and be done with it. You have done what you could. Some blunders, losses, and absurdities no doubt crept in; forget them as soon as you can.

Tomorrow is a new day; let today go so you can begin tomorrow well and serenely, with too high a spirit to be encumbered with your old nonsense. Each new day is too dear, with its hopes and invitations, to waste a moment on yesterdays."

By "old nonsense", Emerson is referring to our worries and woes. The two are synonymous. In the study I cited, nonsense and worry were one and the same thing — not once in a while — but nearly every single time.

I invite you to cut-and-paste the statement and post it where you'll see it at the close of your work day. If you allow Emerson's words to release you completely from your day's labor, your evening is guaranteed to be more enjoyable, more relaxing, and more restorative. You'll also sleep better. I've framed Emerson's statement and placed it on my desk and I read it with conviction before closing up shop for the day. Then I head into the evening committed to being happy and at peace, so I can enjoy the people and things I love.

Chapter 2- Don't Worry About What People May Think

Do you ever find yourself worrying about what people think about you?

Have you ever felt rejected and gotten defensive when someone had criticized something you did or said?

Are there times when you held back on doing something you know could benefit yourself and even others because you were scared about how some people would think or react?

If so, you can consider yourself normal. The desire for connection and to fit in is one of the six basic human needs according to the research of great people such as Tony Robbins and Cloe Madanes. Psychologically, to be rejected by "the tribe" could represent a threat to your survival.

This begs the question: "If wanting people's approval is natural and healthy, is it always a good thing?"

Imagine for a moment if you could, what life would be like if you didn't care so much, about what other people think. Would you be self-centered and egotistical, or would you be set free to live a life fulfilling your true purpose without being held back by a fear of rejection?

For almost my entire life I have been wrestled with caring about other people's opinions.

I thought this made me selfless and considerate. While caring about the opinion of others helped me put myself into other people's shoes, I discovered that my desire, or more specifically my attachment to wanting approval, had the potential to be one of my most selfish and destructive qualities.

Approval Addiction will make you Miserable

If wanting the approval of others is a natural desire, how can it be a problem? The problem is that, like any drug, the high you get from getting approval eventually wears off. If having the approval of others is the only way you know how to feel happy, then you're going to be miserable until you get your next so called "fix."

What this means is that simply wanting approval isn't the problem. The real issue is being too attached to getting approval from others as the only way to feel fulfilled. To put it simply, addiction to approval puts your happiness under the control of others.

Because their happiness depends on others, approval addicts can be the most easily manipulated. I often see this with unhealthy or even abusive relationships. All an abuser has to do is threaten to make the approval addict feel rejected or like they're being selfish, and they'll stay under the abuser's spell.

Approval addiction leads to a lack of boundaries and will ultimately lead to resentment. Many times I felt resentment toward others because they crossed my boundaries, and yet I would remain silent. I didn't want to come across as rude for speaking up about how someone upset me.

The problem is this would lead to pent-up resentment over time because there's a constant feeling that people should just "know better." When I took an honest look at the situation, though, I had to consider whose fault it was if resentment built up because my boundaries were crossed.

Is it the fault of the person who unknowingly crossed those boundaries or the person who failed to enforce boundaries out of fear of rejection?

Looking at my own life, I actually appreciate when someone I care about lets me know I've gone too far. It gives me a chance to make things right. If I don't let others know how they've hurt me because of fear of rejection, aren't I actually robbing them of the opportunity to seek my forgiveness and do better?

This leads me to my final point, approval addiction leads to being selfish. The deception is that the selfishness is often disguised and justified as selflessness.

As a writer, I'm exposed to critics. If I don't overcome a desire for wanting approval from everyone, then their opinions can stop me from sharing something incredibly helpful with those who'd benefit from my work.

Approval addiction is a surefire way to rob the world of your gifts. How selfish is it to withhold what I have to offer to others all because I'm thinking too much about what some people may think of me?

As strange as it sounds, doing things for others can be selfish. On an airplane, they say to put the oxygen mask on yourself before putting it on a child. This is because if the adult passes out trying to help the child, both are in trouble.

In much the same way, approval addiction can lead a person to martyr themselves to the point that everyone involved suffers.

For instance, if a person spends so much time helping others that they neglect their own health, then in the long run, it may be everyone else who has to take care of them when they get sick, causing an unnecessary burden.

Selfless acts, done at the expense of one's greater priorities, can be just as egotistical and destructive as selfish acts.

Overcoming Approval Addiction

The first way to overcome approval addiction is to be gentle with yourself. Wanting to feel connected with others is normal. It's only an issue when it's imbalanced with other priorities like having boundaries.

What approval addicts are often missing is self-approval. We all have an inner critic that says things like, "You're not good enough. You're nothing compared to these people around you. If you give yourself approval, you're being selfish."

You can't get rid of this voice. What you can do is choose whether or not to buy into it or something greater.

You also have a part of yourself that says, "You're worthy. You're good enough. You're just as valuable as anyone else." The question becomes: "Which voice do I choose to align to?"

This often means asking yourself questions like, "Can I give myself some approval right now? What is something I appreciate about myself?" The next step is to then be willing to actually allow yourself to receive that approval.

To break approval addiction, remember to treat yourself the way you want others to treat you.

In much the same way, you can overcome approval addiction by equally valuing other important things, such as your need for significance and control. While wanting to control things can be taken too far just like wanting approval, it is the Yang to approval seeking's Yin. Both are necessary for balance.

Questions that typically help me are: "Do I want other people's opinions to have power over me? Would I rather let this person control me or maintain control over my own life?"

Finally, there is the ultimate key to overcoming approval addiction. It's by using the greatest motivator— unconditional love.

Worrying about what other people think masquerades as love. In reality, when you really love someone, you're willing to have their disapproval.

Imagine a parent with a child. If the parent is too concerned about the child's opinion of them, they might not discipline their child for fear of the child disliking them.

Have you ever seen a parent who lets their child get away with anything because they don't want to be the "bad guy?" Is this truly loving?

To break approval addiction, I realized I had to ask one of the most challenging questions anyone could ask themselves: Am I willing to love this person enough to have them hate me?

If you really care for someone, telling them, "You're screwing up your life" and having them feel the pain of that statement might be the most loving thing you can do.

This comes with the very real possibility they will reject you for pointing out the truth. However, if you love someone, wouldn't you rather have them go through a little short-term pain in order to save them a lot of pain down the road?

On the upside, many people will eventually come to appreciate you more in the long term if you're willing, to be honest with them and prioritize your love for them over your desire for their approval.

If you have to share a harsh truth, a mentor, Andy Benjamin, taught me that you can make this easier by first asking, "Can I be a true friend?" to let them know what you're about to say is coming from a place of love.

I've found that everything, including the desire for approval, can serve or enslave you depending on how you respond to it.

Do you use your desire for approval as a force to help you see things from other people's perspective, or do you use it as a crutch on which you base your happiness?

Do you use your desire for approval as a reminder to give yourself approval, or do you use it as an excuse to be miserable when others don't give you approval?

Finally, are you willing show the ultimate demonstration of genuine love—sacrificing your desire for approval in order to serve another?

Chapter 3- Focus on What You Control. Not What You Can't.

The average person starts the personal development journey in order to gain more control over his or her ability to make changes in their lives. But, somewhere along the journey, they forget that there are certain things we really don't have any control over.

In fact, there are some things that were never meant to be controlled. By focusing on the things we do control, and letting go of the things we don't the ride through the journey of life and personal development tends to be a lot less bumpy.

The Things That We Control

Thoughts

Whether you realize it or not you do have the ability to control your thoughts. The first step is developing an awareness that you do in fact have the ability to control what you are thinking. Unfortunately, advertisers, marketers, and anybody else who has benefited from attempting to exert influence over you have done a pretty good job keeping you unaware. So how do you choose what to think? It's simple. Decide that YOU will be the one that chooses the thoughts and images that will fill your brain, not anybody else. Once you decide, then all you have to do is use empowering questions to control the focus of your mind.

-Emotions

Emotions are largely a byproduct of what you are thinking. If you learn to control your thoughts, your emotions will eventually be under control. Learning to control emotions is important because they are extremely powerful. If there's anything that advertisers have learned it's that associating emotion with one of their products is exactly what you gets you to the next step, which is to take action.

-Actions

If you haven't noticed by now, each one of these builds on the other, and if you don't control one, then you won't control the other. In other words, if you don't control your thoughts and your emotions, your actions will occur on autopilot. Have you ever come from home shopping with what is referred to as an "impulse buy"? This basically occurs because you see something, you have a thought about it, you have the sellers intended emotion, and you take the sellers intended action. Take control and take your intended action.

-Reactions

If there's any phrase that might make you feel like I'm beating the dead horse of personal development it's that "Life is not about what happens to you, but how you react to what happens to you?". I know it's been said over and over again, but it seems to be the root structure of this tree we call personal development. How you react to everything that happens in your life is a choice. Setbacks, wipeouts, and the overall obstacles along the road of life are inevitable. But, how you deal with them will ultimately determine the quality of your life.

-Energy

I have a good friend who is a life coach once told me "assume that everybody you are talking to can feel everything you are thinking." There's no doubt that you feel a vibe from almost anybody you talk to. You've also been in a situation where somebody really liked you right off the bat. The combination of thoughts, emotions, actions, and reactions results in energy, and the energy you give off is something you control. By having a good energy we attract positive experiences and people.

The Things We Don't Control

-People's actions

Let's be honest with ourselves for a moment. As much as we'd like to think we have the ability to control other people's actions, people will ultimately act according to their own will. Unless somebody holds a gun to another person's head the action they take is their choice. We may have the ability to influence another person's action, but we don't control their action.

-People's reactions

Have you ever walked up to somebody in a bar, restaurant or lounge, with a smile on your face and said "hello" only to have them blow you off with a scowl? Have you ever been to a restaurant and had a really obnoxious waiter or waitress? It's likely that you have and if you haven't you will at some point in your life. Most people are going through their own world of problems, and how they react to you often has nothing to do with you. Obviously, this doesn't mean you should have any social boundaries and act like an idiot. But don't take people's reactions personally. You never know what they're going through.

Human nature is to want to force everything. In fact, we have continually invented technologies to speed up certain things in our lives, and in the process, we often forget that there is a divine order in which things occur. The power of presence is another mantra that seems to be echoed throughout the personal development community. While the fact that you are exactly where you are supposed to be, experiencing exactly what you are supposed to be experiencing, doing exactly what you are supposed to be doing, may sometimes be disconcerting, it is a fact of life. An attempt to control divine order is an exercise in futility.

Let nature take its course. When you plant a seed, you don't dig it up to see how well it's growing. That would be completely silly and you would end up starting the process all over again with a new seed. It seems to me that manifesting things into our lives works in a similar manner. Every time we questions where the thing we asked for is, it's like digging up the seeds.

Focus your efforts on the things you do control, let go of the things you don't control, and you will find yourself in a much more peaceful, zen-like state of mind.

Chapter 4- Try to be in The Moment

.

How can you bring calm and peace to the middle of a stressful and chaotic day?

The answer is simple, though not always so easy to put into practice: learn to be present.

No matter how out-of-control your day is, no matter how stressful your job or life becomes, the act of being present can become an oasis. It can change your life, and it's incredibly simple.

When I asked people what things prevent them from having a peaceful day, some of the responses:

Work, the internet, my own lizard brain.

Social media and other digital distractions.

For me, it's too many things coming at me all at once. Whether it's news or decisions, or work to be done.

My children.

Dishes, Laundry, Taking trash out.

Needless interruptions.

Lack of control. I own a business, and often "urgent" things will come up that need to be investigated/fixed right away (their definition, not necessarily mine).

My own monkey mind.

The amazing thing: all of these problems can be solved by one technique. Being Present.

How Being Present Solves Problems

When you look at all of the problems above, you can see if you look closely that the problems are entirely in the mind. Sure, there are external forces at work: an uncontrollable job, the stress of kids and chores and interruptions and digital distractions. But it's how our mind handles those external forces that are the problem.

If you are completely present, the external forces are no longer a problem, because there is only you and that external force, in this moment, and not a million other things you need to worry about.

If your kid interrupts you, you can stress out because you have other things to worry about and now your kid is adding to your worries or interrupting your calm. Or you can be present, and there is then only you and the child. You can appreciate that child for who he/she is, and be grateful you have this moment with him/her.

If your job demands that you focus on an urgent task, you can stress out because you have a million other things to do and not enough time to do them. Or you can be present, and focus completely on that task, and now there is only that one task and you. When you're done, you can move on to the next task.

Social media and other digital distractions don't interrupt us if we close them and learn to pour ourselves completely into the present task. And if we need to do email, Twitter, or read blogs, we can set aside everything else and just be present with that one digital task.

Being present becomes, then, a way to handle any problem, any distraction, any stressor. It allows everything else to fade away, leaving only you and whatever you're dealing with right now.

How to Practice Being Present

The method for being present is fairly simple, but it's the practice that matters most.

Most people don't learn to be present because they don't practice, not because it's so hard to do.

When you practice something regularly, you become good at it. It becomes more a mode of being, rather than a task on your to-do list.

Practice, practice, and being present will become natural.

Here's how to do it: whatever you're doing, right now, learn to focus completely on doing that one thing. Pay attention: to every aspect of what you're doing, to your body, to the sensations, to your thoughts.

You will notice your thoughts, if you're paying attention, jump to other things. That's OK — you are not trying to force all other thoughts from your mind. But by becoming aware of that jumping around in your thoughts, you have found the tool for gently bringing yourself back to your present task. Just notice the jumping thoughts, and lovingly come back.

Do this once, then do it again. Don't worry about how many times you must do it. Just do it now.

It can become tiring at first if you're not used to it. Don't worry about that. Let yourself rest if you grow tired. Come back and practice again in a little while. It's not meant to be exhausting — instead, you should notice how your worries melt away and you enjoy your present task much more.

Be joyful in whatever you're doing, grateful that you're able to do that task, and fully appreciate every little movement and tactile sensation of the task. You'll learn that anything can be an amazing experience, anything can be a miracle.

Practice throughout your day, every day. Little "mindfulness bells" are useful to remind you to come back to the present. Thich Nhat Hanh once recommended that stoplights be your mindfulness bell as you drive. You can find mindfulness bells everywhere: your child's voice, your co-workers appearing before you, a regular event on your computer, the noise of traffic.

Meditation is a fantastic way to practice, only because it removes much of the complexity of the world and allows you to just learn to be aware of your mind and to bring yourself back to the present moment. It's not complicated: meditation can be done anywhere, anytime. A meditation teacher is useful if you can find one.

Practice, repeatedly, in small easy beautiful steps. Each step is a wonder in itself, and each practice helps you to find that calm in the middle of the traffic of your life.

'Drink your tea slowly and reverently, as if it is the axis on which the world earth revolves – slowly, evenly, without rushing toward the future. Live the actual moment.

Only this moment is life.' ~Thich Nhat Hanh

Chapter 5- Tips to Overcome Negative Thoughts and Worry

"See the positive side, the potential, and make an effort."
~Dalai Lama

Even though I meditate and do yoga every other day, I still sometimes fall prey to negative thinking. Having negative thoughts play out like a movie can only bring you pain, something that I've experienced many times throughout my life.

Negative thoughts will drain you of energy and keep you from being in the present moment. The more you give in to your negative thoughts, the stronger they become. I like the imagery of a small ball rolling along the ground, and as it rolls, it becomes bigger and faster.

That's what one small negative thought can turn into a huge, speeding ball of ugliness. On the contrary, a small positive thought can have the same effect blossoming into a beautiful outcome.

When we start to have negative thoughts, it's hard to stop them. And it's much easier said than done to shift your focus to positive thoughts. But it's the only way, especially if you want to avoid going down a path that is painful and unnecessary.

Way's to overcome negative thoughts that you can also try

Smile.

If I don't do much of this during the week, I will literally bring myself in front of a mirror and force myself to smile. It really does help change your mood and relieve stress. I also feel lighter because it takes fewer muscles to smile than to frown.

Meditate or do yoga.

One of the first things I did was head to a yoga class. It took my focus away from my thoughts and brought my attention to my breath. Yoga is also very relaxing, which helped ease my mind. Yoga helped me stay present to my experience so instead of jumping to what could happen, it brought me back to the now—the only moment, the most important moment.

Surround yourself with positive people.

I called a friend who I knew could give me constructive yet loving feedback. When you're stuck in a negative spiral, talk to people who can put things into perspective and won't feed your negative thinking

Change the tone of your thoughts from negative to positive.

For example, instead of thinking, "We are going to have a hard time adjusting to some living situations," think, "I will face some challenges in my living situation, but I will come up with solutions that I will be happy with."

Help someone.

Take the focus away from you and do something nice for another person. I decided to make a tray of food and donate it to the Salvation Army. It took my mind off of things and I felt better for helping someone else.

Remember that no one is perfect and let yourself move forward.

It's easy to dwell on your mistakes. I feel terrible that I acted a certain way or that I hurt someone. The only thing I can do now is to learn from my mistakes and move forward. I definitely don't want to keep dwelling on it.

Don't play the victim. You create your life—take responsibility.

If you find yourself caught in negative thinking and you begin to feel stuck.Even if our living situation becomes unbearable, there is always a way out. You will always have the choice to make change happen if need be.

Sing.

I don't remember lyrics very well and it's probably the reason that I don't enjoy singing, but every time I do sing I always feel better. When we sing, we show our feelings and this provides an amazing stress relief.

List five things that you are grateful for right now.

Being grateful helps appreciate what you already have. Here's my list: my kids,family, health,job that I love, a six-week trip to Asia, a new yoga class that I'll be starting, and for my mom's biopsy coming out clean.

Read positive quotes.

I like to place Post-It notes with positive quotes on my computer, fridge door, and mirror as reminders to stay positive. Also, I'd like to share with you a quote by an unknown author that was shared in a meditation class that I attended:

Watch your thoughts, they become words.

Watch your words, they become actions.

Watch your actions, they become habits.

Watch your habits, they become your character.

Watch your character, it becomes your destiny.

Chapter 6- Be with Positive People

In our everyday life, we are surrounded by a wide variety of people. Some of the people we deal with on a daily basis are a joy to be with, and just their loving presence nurtures and encourages us. Others seem to have the opposite effect: draining us of our positive energy, making us feel tired and exhausted through constant emotional bullying and manipulation. We must refuse to allow ourselves to be treated poorly. Our well-being is definitely easily influenced by those around us, and if we can keep this in mind, we will have greater insights into the quality of our social interactions and their energetic effect on us.

Equally, every move we ourselves make has an effect that touches all the people around us. On an even more subtle level, when we share space with another person, we often pick up on their energy, feeling how they feel and attuning to them, whether we mean to or not. This is what we mean when we say a mood or a feeling is contagious.

Once we think more deeply about the people we interact with, it becomes easier for us to work toward filling our lives with people who help us to cultivate healthy and positive relationships. Obviously, it is not always possible - for example at work - to choose the people we spend time, but in our personal lives, we can take control over the right people with whom to surround ourselves.

All we have to do is take a few moments to reflect on how another person makes us feel. Assessing the people we spend the most time with, allows us to see if they add something constructive to, or subtract from, our lives. If a friend saps our strength, for example, we can simply decide to tell them how we feel or else spend less time with them.

We will find that the moment we are honest with ourselves about our own feelings, the more candid we can be with others about how they make us feel. While this may involve some drastic changes to our social life, it can bring about a personal transformation that will truly empower us, since the decision to live our truth will infuse our lives with greater happiness.

When we surround ourselves with positive people, we clear away the negativity that exists around us and creates more room to welcome nurturing and renewed energy. Doing this not only enriches our lives, but also envelops us in a supportive and healing space that fosters greater growth, understanding, and love of ourselves - as well as those we care about.

Choose your friends with care - they create the environment in which you will either thrive or wilt. Give everyone the opportunity to be a friend, but share your dreams and goals only with those who value them as much as you do.

"People are like dirt. They can either nourish you and help you grow as a person, or they can stunt your growth and make you wilt and die." ~ Plato

Reasons to surround yourself with happy people

Let yourself be lifted up by the positive vibes of others.

Some people seem to struggle each day to find contentment or a happy way of living, while others easily face each day with spirit. Have you ever thought about which type of person you are? Or how this might describe those around you? There's value in surrounding yourself with people who know how to lift their own spirits – which means they'll probably lift yours, too! It's one of our favorite tips for learning how to be happier.

Happiness is contagious:

 One of the best ways to find happiness is to find those who know how to nurture and create their own happiness and share it freely. Spend time around these people and you'll find yourself seeing the world differently.

Laughter is a great way to bond with others:

A great way to connect with others is to share laughter or spend time having fun with them. Watching how someone reacts to a funny situation and feeling yourself pulled into the good humor, is a great way to bond and get to know each other better.

Less complaining is good for everyone:

We all know life can be hard. We all have our struggles. But isn't it refreshing to spend time with people who don't waste time and energy complaining? You can almost feel your spirits lifting around someone who is willing to see the good in things.

Learn coping strategies:

We all have our strategies for dealing with hard days and rough times. But it can't hurt to take inspiration from those around you. They may have ideas you haven't considered. Better yet, you might be invited to join them! Their evening walks or bookstore wanderings may become your new favorite outlet on stressful days.

We become like those we keep closest:

There's an old saying that we become like those we choose to hold closest. Look around at your inner circle of friends and confidantes. Are they who you would like to become? Do you admire and respect them? If not, perhaps you should consider why you don't and open your circle to new inspiration.

It's worth the time it may take to consciously surround yourself with people who can create goodness for themselves, and those around them. Take a look around you and see – do you seem to be drawn to happy people? Why or why not?

"Love yourself—accept yourself—forgive yourself—and be good to yourself, because without you the rest of us are without a source of many wonderful things." ~Leo F. Buscaglia

Love yourself.

Despite all the things that you think may be terribly wrong with you, love yourself. Love yourself.

Tattoo it on your brain.

I can think of so many reasons why you should love yourself, but here's just one: It is incredibly dull and uninspiring to be around people who do not love themselves.

I spent many years beating myself up and feeling like I was a monster. I'm sure I was not much fun to be around and I also know that I didn't feel like I was worthy or deserving of the jobs I was trying to land. It is very challenging to hire someone or love someone who fights you by holding up a mirror of hatred toward themselves.

Here's my challenge for you today: Take a picture of your face and remember that in 10 years time you will be amazed at how gorgeous you were. Be amazed now.

Identify something about you that you may not adore and find a way to at least laugh at it or like it, even a little bit.

We all have parts of our body that we would like to change or we may feel embarrassed about.However,Everyone is in the same boat and I have learned that I can make light of everything or sit home and feel sorry for myself ,which benefits no one.

Either way, the choice is yours to make.

Forgive yourself.

I have attended meditation workshops on forgiveness, and every time, without fail, people start crying. Almost everyone in the room will have at least shed a tear. This leads me to believe that we are all indeed connected, a union—which is what the word Yoga means.

The human experience is so similar, and yes, I know the details are vastly different, and that the devil lies in the details, but we still share the same weight on our shoulders. That weight would be diminished if we chose to forgive instead of harboring guilt or anger.

People cry most in my workshops when we do the meditation on forgiving yourself. Most likely it's because we are hardest on ourselves.

What can you forgive yourself for today?

I forgive myself for not being perfect.

This shift occurred was when I was finally able to understand I don't need to be perfect. We often hold ourselves to impossible standards and end up feeling bad.

Ask yourself honestly, "What can I forgive myself for?"

Sometimes it takes simply saying it aloud or writing it down to realize that you actually no longer need to bear the brunt of it.

3. Be good to yourself. Do things that you inspire you daily.

Make a list. Grab your iPad or your notepad or even your hand and draw up a list of things you can do today to make you feel good.

Keep adding to the list. Forgive yourself if you skip a couple and love yourself no matter how long or short the list is and how much you accomplish on it.

You will not be graded or tested on this list.

My list involves a lot of laughing. My "Feel Good" list also has: my yoga classes, writing, a long leisurely dinner with friends, having a great glass of wine, staying up all night reading a book I cannot put down, being with kids who have special needs and teaching them poetry, Modern

Family, video calling with my nephews, and the list goes on.

Do something every single day that makes you feel good, whether it is changing your thought patterns or taking a bath while reading a magazine in the tub.

Maybe it's getting an extra hour of sleep or staying up late and watching Pretty Woman for the 100th time.

Pleasure and joy are highly underrated and beating ourselves, up highly overrated. Flip it! Cultivate the opposite.

One of my main rules for myself is that if you fall, you must laugh about it, which cultivates a sense of humor, and hopefully a little joy. You need at least a little joy daily. Sprinkle it on your cereal, slip it in your downward facing dog, add it to your pinot noir.

Accept that you are indeed the source of many wonderful things. If you need help remembering what they are from time to time, keep making your feel good lists. Keep coming back to the love that is inherently yours. It is your birthright. And so it is.

Whatever it takes. Just do it.

A good friend told me after she returned from a yoga retreat that she wanted to live her life every day as if she was still on the retreat. And why shouldn't she? What a revelation! What a revolution of the mind.

Be good to yourself. You will train other people to do the same.

And guess what? If they aren't good to you, you will still have your old standby who is always good to you: YOU. Pretty much what matters most at the end of the day. You being good to you. The rest will follow.

Remember the 90's En Vogue song, with the lyrics "Free your mind, the rest will follow"?

It will. So get up and dance.

Chapter 8- What Happens When We Exercise and How It Makes Us Happier

Exercise has been touted to be a cure for nearly everything in life, from depression to memory loss, Alzheimer's disease, Parkinson's and more. At the same time, similar to the topic of sleep, I found myself having very little specific and scientific knowledge about what exercise really does to our bodies and our brains.

"Yes, yes, I know all about it, that's the thing with the endorphins, that makes you feel good and why we should exercise and stuff, right?" is what I can hear myself say to someone bringing this up. I would pick up things here and there, yet really digging into the connection of exercise and how it effects us has never been something I've done.

Inspired by a recent post from Joel on what makes us happy I've set out to uncover the connection between our feeling of happiness and exercising regularly.

What triggers happiness in our brain when we exercise?

Most of us are aware of what happens to the body when we exercise. We build more muscle or more stamina. We feel how daily activities like climbing stairs becomes easier if we exercise regularly. When it comes to our brain and mood though, the connection isn't so clear.

The line around our "endorphins are released" is more something I throw around to sound smart, without really knowing what it means. Here is what actually happens:

If you start exercising, your brain recognizes this as a moment of stress. As your heart pressure increases, the brain thinks you are either fighting the enemy or fleeing from it. To protect yourself and your brain from stress, you release a protein called BDNF (Brain-Derived Neurotrophic Factor). This BDNF has a protective and also reparative element to your memory neurons and acts as a reset switch. That's why we often feel so at ease and things are clear after exercising and eventually happy.

At the same time, endorphins, another chemical to fight stress, is released in your brain. Your endorphins main purpose is this writes researcher McGovern:

These endorphins tend to minimize the discomfort of exercise, block the feeling of pain and are even associated with a feeling of euphoria.

Overall, there is a lot going on inside our brain and it is in fact oftentimes a lot more active than when we are just sitting down or actually concentrating mentally:

So, BDNF and endorphins are the reasons exercise makes us feel so good. The somewhat scary part is that they have a very similar and addictive behavior like morphine, heroin or nicotine. The only difference? Well, it's actually good for us.

The key to maximizing happiness through exercise: don't do more, but focus on when

Now here is where it all gets interesting now. We know the basic foundations of why exercising makes us happy and what happens inside our brain cells. The most important part to uncover now is of course how we can trigger this in an optimal and longer lasting way.

A recent study from Penn State university shed some light on the matter and the results are more than surprising.

They found that to be more productive and happier on a given work day, it doesn't matter so much, if you work-out regularly, if you haven't worked out on that particular day:

"Those who had exercised during the preceding month but not on the day of testing generally did better on the memory test than those who had been sedentary, but did not perform nearly as well as those who had worked out that morning."

New York Times best-selling author Gretchen Reynolds has written a whole book about the subject matter titled "The first 20 minutes". To get the highest level of happiness and benefits for health, the key is not to become a professional athlete. On the contrary, a much smaller amount is needed to reach the level where happiness and productivity in everyday life peaks:

"The first 20 minutes of moving around, if someone has been really sedentary, provide most of the health benefits. You get prolonged life, reduced disease risk — all of those things come in in the first 20 minutes of being active."

So really, you can relax and don't have to be on the look-out for the next killer work-out. All you have to do is get some focused 20 minutes in to get the full happiness boost every day:

"On exercise days, people's mood significantly improved after exercising. Mood stayed about the same on days they didn't, with the exception of people's sense of calm which deteriorated." (University of Bristol)

How to get into a consistent exercise habit: The dance with the endorphins

Now, that's all nice to hear you might say, starting to exercise regularly or even daily is still easier written than done. At end of the day, there is quite a lot of focus required to help you get into the habit of exercising daily. The most important part to note first is that exercise is a "keystone" habit according to Charles Duhigg, New York Times bestselling author of "The Power of Habit: Why We Do What We Do in Life and Business". This means that daily exercise can pave the way not only for happiness but also growth in all other areas of your life.

In a recent post from Joel, he wrote about the power of daily exercise for his everyday life. Coincidentally, he follows the above rules very accurately and exercises daily before doing anything else. He writes:

By 9:45am, I've done an hour of coding on the most important task I have right now on Buffer, I've been to the gym and had a great session, and I've done 30 minutes of emails. It's only 9:45am and I've already succeeded, and I feel fantastic.

I've spoken lots to Joel about his habit of exercising and here are some of the most important things to do, in order to set yourself up for success and make your daily exercise fun:

Put your gym clothes right over your alarm clock or phone when you go to bed: This technique sounds rather simple but has been one of the most powerful ones. If you put everything the way you want it for the gym before you go to sleep and put your alarm under your gym clothes, you will have a much easier time to convince yourself to put your gym clothes on.

Track your exercises and log them at the same time after every exercise: When you try to exercise regularly, the key is to make it a habit. One way to achieve this is to create a so-called "reward", that will remind you of the good feelings you get from exercising. In our big list of top web apps, we have a full section on fitness apps that might be handy. Try out Fitocracy orRunKeeper to log your workouts. Try to have a very clear logging process in place. Log your workout just before you go into the shower or exactly when you walk out of the gym.

Think about starting small and then start even smaller: Here is a little secret. When I first started exercising, I did it with 5 minutes per day, 3 times a week. Can you imagine that? 5 minutes of timed exercise, 3 times a week? That's nothing you might be thinking. And you are right because the task is so easy and anyone can succeed with it, you can really start to make a habit out of it. Try no more than 5 or 10 minutes if you are getting started.

There are lots more great ideas for how you can create a habit from Joel in his post on the exercise habit, be sure to check it out, it might be a lot of help here. I am sure that if you dedicate just very little time, you can get into an awesome exercise routine that makes you happier, more productive and relaxed than ever before.

Quick last fact: You get the highest level of happiness with exercise if you are just starting out

As a quick last fact, exercise, the increase of the BDNF proteins in your brain acts as a mood enhancer. The effects are similar to drug addiction one study found. So when you start exercising, the feeling of euphoria is the highest:

"The release of endorphins has an addictive effect, and more exercise is needed to achieve the same level of euphoria over time." (McGovern)

So this means that if you have never exercised before or not for a long time, your happiness gains will be the highest if you start now.

Chapter 9- How Meditation will Help Anxiety

Fear is almost always just a negative emotion unless on the rare occasion you're facing an actual threat and need to either fight or flee. The usefulness of fear is really minimal in everyday life, particularly when it's in the form of anxiety.Very Stressful events will produce short-term anxiety in almost everyone, which will disappear after the actual event. But for an estimated seven million Americans with some sort of an Anxiety Disorder , anxiety is a chronic condition which is extremely hard to shut off. All of us have friends or family we view as "born worriers," but their reality is can more debilitating than this title describes. Being always in a state of chronic anxiety can and will severely limit their daily activity.

You probably know already if you worry excessively. In fact, if you have chronic anxiety, even the smallest thing can trigger it. You find yourself with fearful thoughts about finances, family, your health, and what's happening at work. Some days you'd rather lie in bed and hide under the covers.

Why You Worry

The first thing to realize is that reality isn't what's actually worrying you, but it's your fixed habit of mind that's causing you to respond to everything with anxiety. Second, you need to look rationally at the anxiety response and understand that you will not improve it by feeling anxious. This seems obvious to non-worriers, but somewhere inside, many "born worriers" believe they are taking care of situations that others are overlooking, like whether they remembered to lock up the house or turn off the gas stove. Any trigger can provoke worry, so the question is how to prevent this from happening.

The Toll it Takes

Because of the mind-body connection, you should also consider the physical side of anxiety. Even if you have accepted worry as a tolerable trait, it exacts a price in the form of insomnia, easy startle response, fatigue, irritability, muscle tension, headaches, inability to relax, trembling, twitching, feeling out of breath, and various stomach and digestive problems. If these persist for more than six months after something bad has happened to you, a diagnosis of a type of anxiety disorder may be appropriate. Even if your symptoms seem manageable, you shouldn't have to live this way. Anticipating the worst, which has become a habit even when no threat is in sight, distorts how you approach work, family, and the world in general.

There are many theories about what causes chronic anxiety, but they are as diverse as explanations for depression. It's more useful to consider how to retrain your mind so that your worry subsides and is replaced by a normal undisturbed mood. The standard medical advice is to take medication (usually some form of tranquilizer), augmented by talking to a therapist. However, self-care has other tools, such as meditation, diet, sleep, massage, and exercise that you can pursue on your own.

Meditation

One aspect of anxiety is racing thoughts that won't go away. Meditation helps with this part of the problem by quieting the overactive mind. Instead of buying into your fearful thoughts, you can start identifying with the silence that exists between every mental action. Through regular practice, you experience that you're not simply your thoughts and feelings. You can detach yourself from these to rest in your own being. This involves remaining centered, and if a thought or outside trigger pulls you out of your center, your meditation practice allows you to return there again.

Being able to center yourself is a skill that anyone can learn, once they have the intention and the experience of what it feels like. Anxious people often shy away from meditation for various reasons. "I can't meditate" is code for feeling too restless to sit still or having too many thoughts while trying to meditate. With a patient teacher, these objections can be overcome. Anyone can meditate, even if the first sessions are short and need to be guided. Being on tranquilizers, which for some anxious people is the only way they can cope, isn't a block to meditation.

Numerous scientific studies have found meditation to be effective for treating anxiety. One study, published in the Psychological Bulletin, combined the findings from over 150 different studies. The overall conclusion was that practicing mindfulness or meditation produced beneficial results, with a substantial improvement in areas like negative personality traits, anxiety, and stress. Another study focused on a wide range of anxiety, from cancer patients to those with social anxiety disorder, and found mindfulness to be an effective management tool.

The researchers analyzed 40 studies totaling 1,120 participants and discovered that the anxiety-reducing benefits from mindfulness might be enjoyed across such a wide range of conditions because when someone learns mindfulness, they learn how to work with difficult and stressful situations.

All mental activity has to have a physical correlation in the brain, and this aspect has been studied in relation to anxiety. Chronic worriers often display increased reactivity in the amygdala, the area of the brain associated with regulating emotions, including fear. Neuroscientists at Stanford University found that people who practiced mindfulness meditation for eight weeks were more able to turn down the reactivity of this area. Other researchers from Harvard found that mindfulness can physically reduce the number of neurons in this fear-triggering part of the brain.

Conclusion

It's difficult to stop worrying sometimes, especially in a world that throws so many problems at us every day, whether they are work-related, health-related or personal. Unfortunately, however, worrying does nothing to help alleviate our stress, but instead, acts as an aggravator of all of our anxieties and insecurities and it helps fuel our negative thoughts. Anyone can see that this is not good for our mental health, personal calm or overall happiness, but how do we shut down our thoughts and just stop? It is possible to change the way you think and turn it around, so that you become a positive person, instead of a negative one. Worrying can also be stopped, or at least, reduced, with a myriad of benefits for your well-being and that of those around you. This e-book was written especially for those who are looking for these answers and who are trying to stop themselves from stressing over all the details of their lives. By following the guidelines in this book, you will be able to achieve a sense of inner calm, gain a more positive outlook on life, and become a lighter, happier person who worries less or not at all. The secret is in your mentality, which can be changed and it all stands in your power. You are the only one who can do something to change your own life and achieve the mental peace you have been craving. All the help and guidance you need can be found in these steps and valuable advice that will prove indispensable in your journey towards positivity. Life is too short to be worrying about it all the time and while you cannot influence the outcome of the things happening around you by worrying about them, you can change the way you feel and the way you approach life and the problems that may appear along the way. Patience, an open mind and a strong will to change your life are the things that you will need, and with the help of this book, you are sure to achieve the results you have been waiting for. Your future peaceful, positive life lies ahead of you.

If you got value from this book.I would love you to leave a review on amazon.Thank you and good luck

Printed in Poland
by Amazon Fulfillment
Poland Sp. z o.o., Wrocław